John Thompson's Modern Course for the Piano — THIRD GRADE

CHRISTMAS PIANO SOLOS

ISBN 978-1-4234-5691-9

WILLIS MUSIC

EXCLUSIVELY DISTRIBUTED BY

HAL•LEONARD®

7777 W. BLUEMOUND RD. P.O. BOX 13819 MILWAUKEE, WI 53213

© 2008 by The Willis Music Co.
International Copyright Secured   All Rights Reserved

Visit Hal Leonard Online at
www.halleonard.com

Contents

Wonderful Christmastime

Use with John Thompson's Modern Course for the Piano
THIRD GRADE BOOK, after page 3.

Words and Music by
Paul McCartney
Arranged by Glenda Austin

Brightly, with a light Rock feel

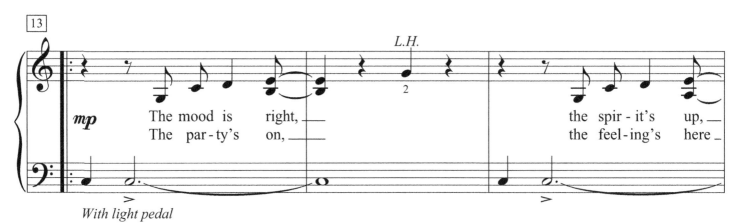

The mood is right, ___ the spir-it's up, ___
The par-ty's on, ___ the feel-ing's here ___

With light pedal

we're here to - night,___
that on - ly comes___

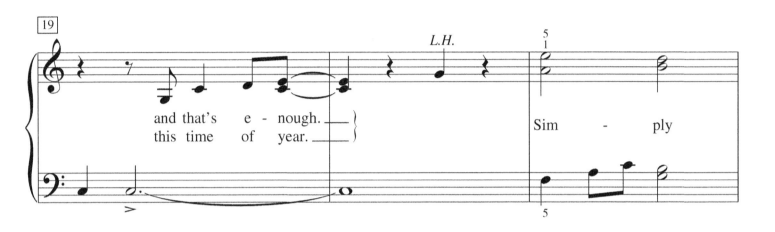

and that's e - nough.___
this time of year.___

Sim - ply

hav - ing a won - der-ful Christ-mas - time.

Sim - ply

hav - ing a won - der - ful Christ - mas - time.

1.

You're All I Want for Christmas

Use after page 11.

Words and Music by Glen Moore
and Seger Ellis
Arranged by Glenda Austin

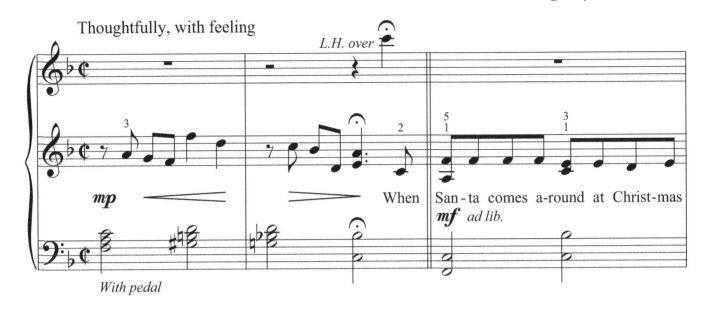

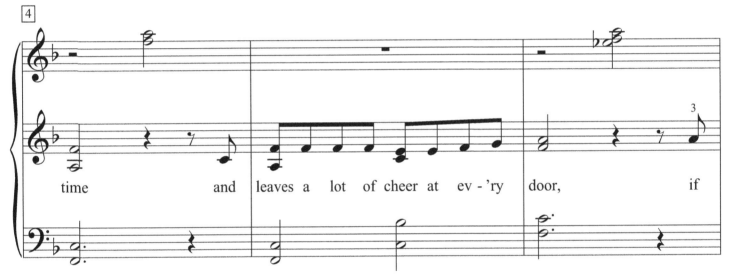

Flowing

più mosso

more. You're all I want for Christ- mas,

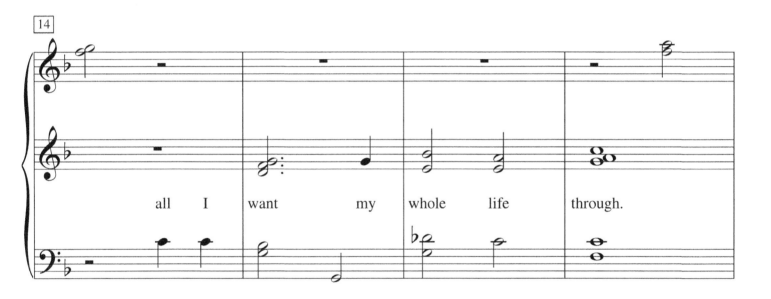

all I want my whole life through.

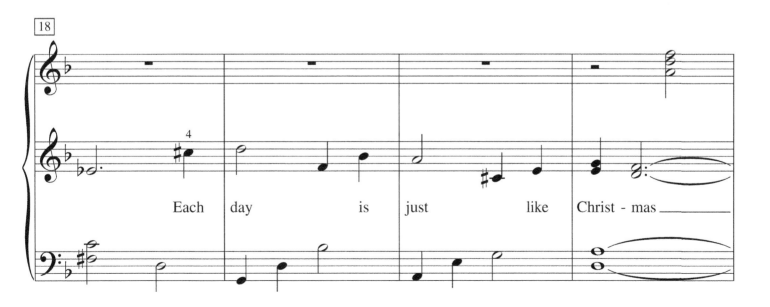

Each day is just like Christ - mas

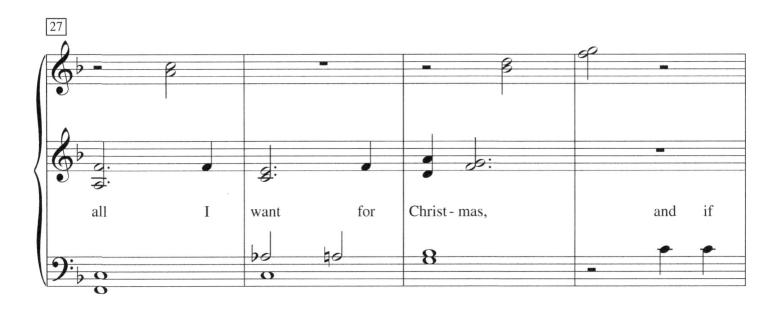

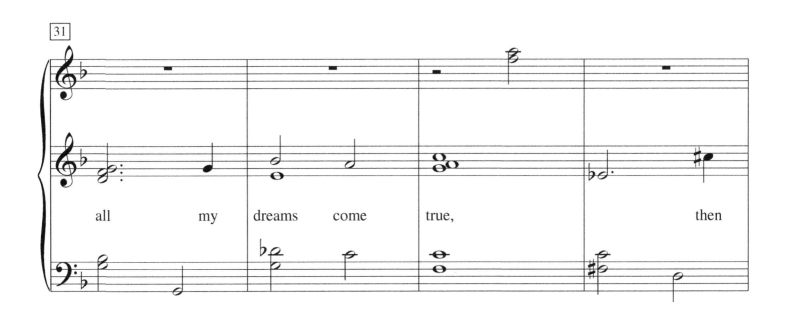

I'll a - wake on Christ - mas morn - ing and find

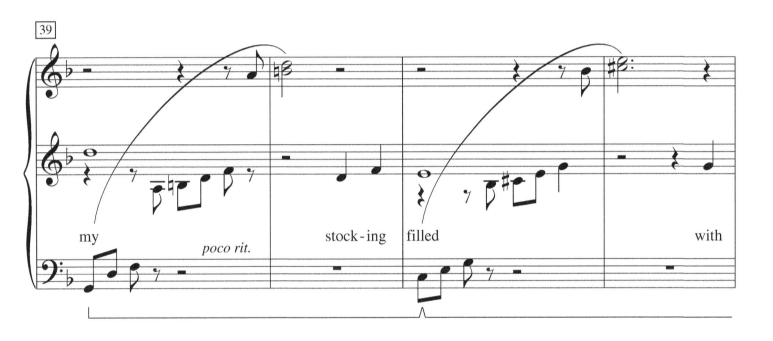

my *poco rit.* stock-ing filled with

you.
a tempo

poco rit.

R.H.

It's Beginning to Look Like Christmas

Use after page 18.

By Meredith Willson
Arranged by Glenda Austin

21 Dolls that will talk and will go for a walk is the hope of Jan-ice and Jen; and

23 Mom and Dad can hard-ly wait for school to start a-gain. *mp*

f

25 It's be-gin-ning to look a lot like *f*

28 Christ-mas ev-'ry-where you go. There's a

31 tree in the grand ho-tel, one in the park as well, the

I'll Be Home for Christmas

Use after page 24.

Words and Music by Kim Gannon
and Walter Kent
Arranged by Glenda Austin

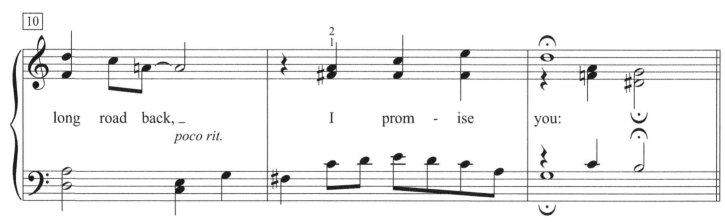

I'll   be   home   for   Christ -   mas, _____

you   can   count   on   me.

Please   have   snow   and   mis -   tle -   toe   and

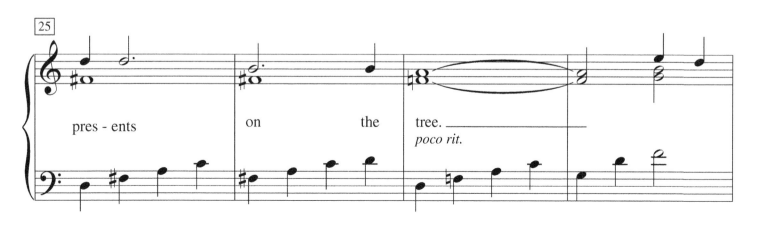

pres - ents   on   the   tree. _____

Christ - mas Eve will find me

a tempo

where the love - light gleams.

I'll be home for Christ - mas, if

f

poco rit.

on - ly in my dreams.

rit.

p

Carol of the Bells

Use after page 41.

Ukrainian Christmas Carol
Arranged by Glenda Austin

With quiet energy

cresc. poco a poco

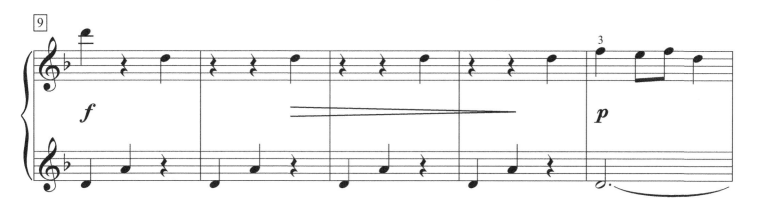

The Most Wonderful Day of the Year

Use after page 49.

Music and Lyrics by Johnny Marks
Arranged by Glenda Austin

We're on the is - land of Mis - fit Toys,

here we don't want to stay. _____

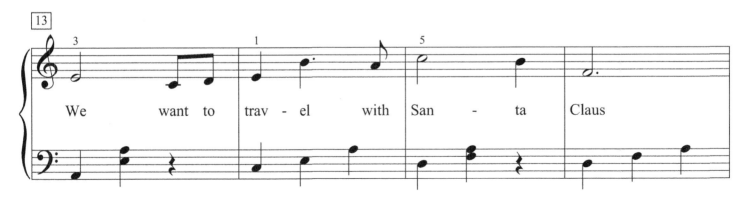

We want to trav - el with San - ta Claus

in his mag - ic sleigh. _____ A

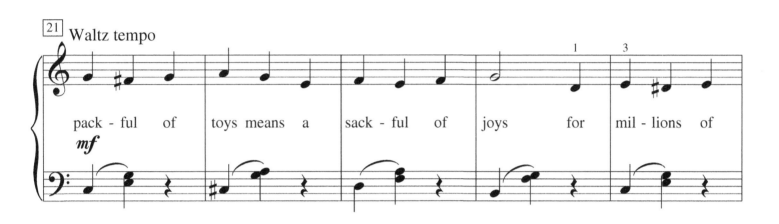

Waltz tempo

pack - ful of toys means a sack - ful of joys for mil - lions of

girls and for mil - lions of boys, when Christ - mas Day is

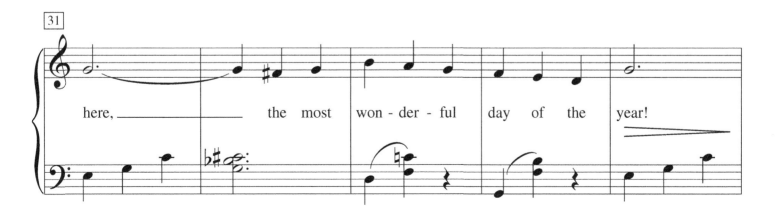

here, _____ the most won - der - ful day of the year!

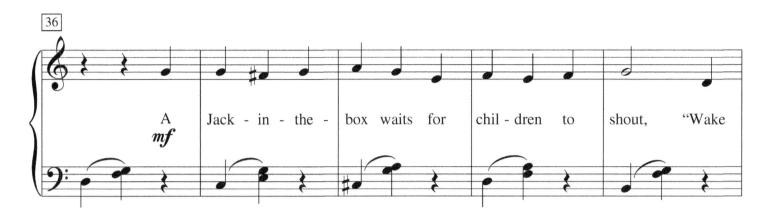

A Jack - in - the - box waits for chil - dren to shout, "Wake

up, don't you know that it's time to come out!" When Christ - mas

Day is here, _____ the most won - der - ful day of the

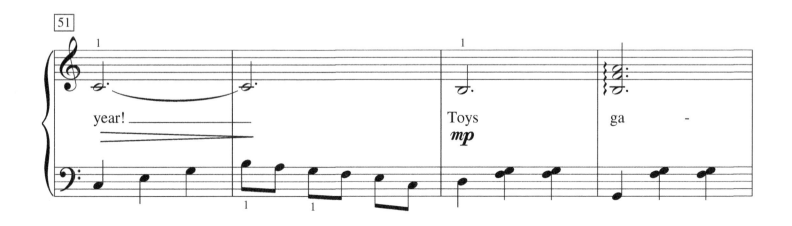

year! _____ Toys ga -

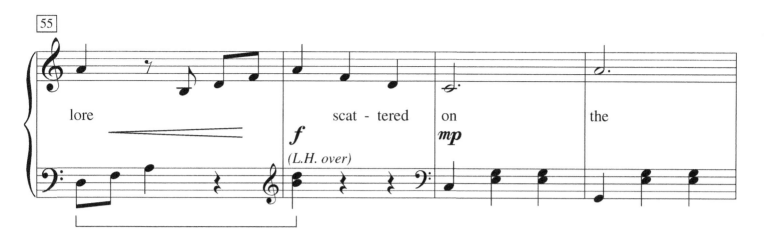

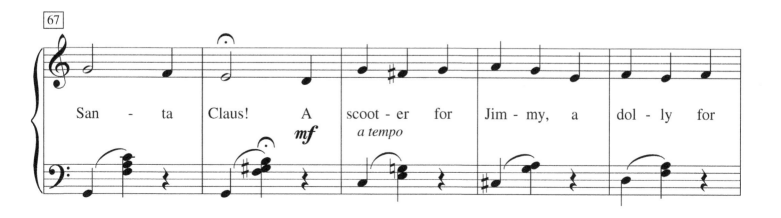

Sue, the kind that will e - ven say, "How do ya do!" When

Christ - mas Day is here, _____ the most won - der - ful,

won - der - ful, won - der - ful, won - der - ful, won - der - ful day of the

broadening

year.

a tempo

f

Pat-a-Pan
(Willie, Take Your Little Drum)
Use after page 57.

Words and Music by
Bernard de la Monnoye
Arranged by Glenda Austin

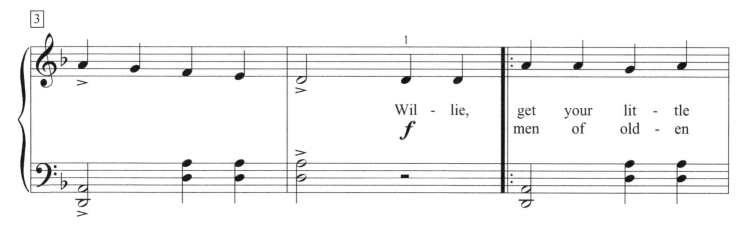

joy - ous tune play on! Tu - re - lu - re - lu, pat - a - pat - a -

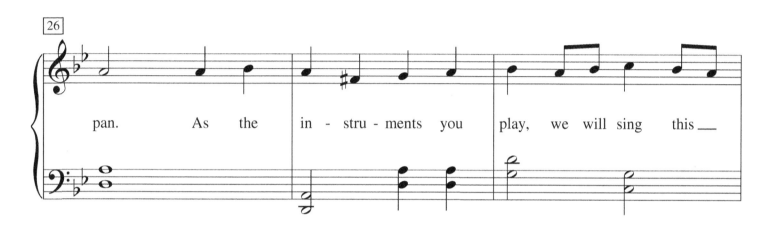

pan. As the in - stru - ments you play, we will sing this ___

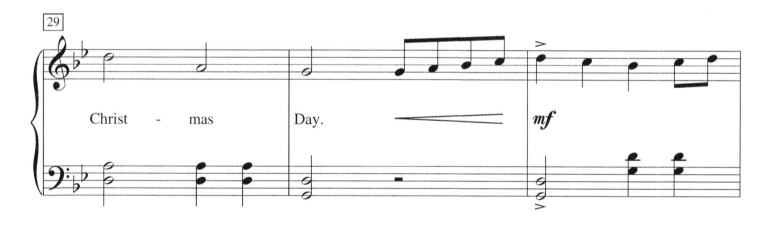

Christ - mas Day. *mf*

pp

Jingle-Bell Rock

Use after page 61.

Words and Music by Joe Beal
and Jim Boothe
Arranged by Glenda Austin

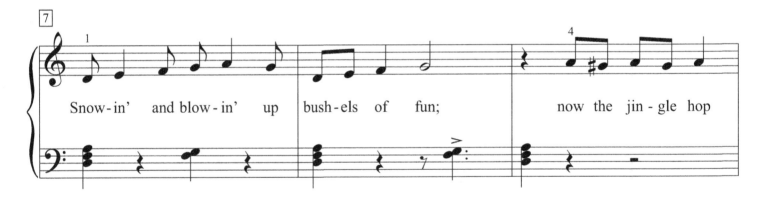

pick up your feet,   jin - gle   a - round the ___   clock.

Mix   and   min - gle   in   a   jin - gl - in' beat,   that's the jin - gle - bell,

that's the jin - gle - bell,   that's the jin - gle - bell   rock. _____

(That's the jin - gle - bell   rock!)   Yeah!

8vb

Merry Christmas, Darling

Use after page 65.

Words and Music by Richard Carpenter
and Frank Pooler
Arranged by Glenda Austin

With great feeling

A Marshmallow World

Use after page 77.

Words by Carl Sigman
Music by Peter De Rose
Arranged by Glenda Austin

Not too fast, liltingly

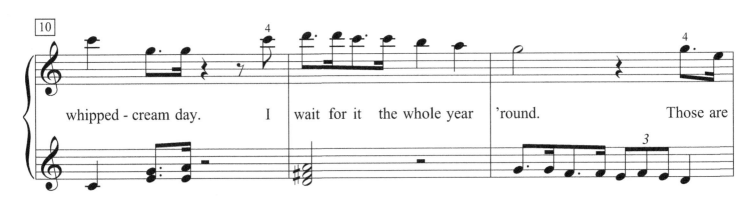

CLASSICAL PIANO SOLOS
Original Keyboard Pieces from Baroque to the 20th Century

JOHN THOMPSON'S MODERN COURSE FOR THE PIANO
Compiled and edited by Philip Low, Sonya Schumann, and Charmaine Siagian

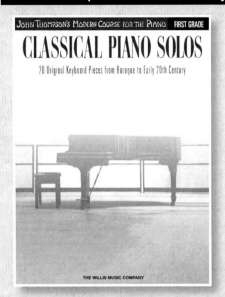

First Grade

22 pieces: *Bartók*: A Conversation • *Mélanie Bonis*: Miaou! Ronron! • *Burgmüller*: Arabesque • *Handel*: Passepied • *d'Indy*: Two-Finger Partita • *Köhler*: Andantino • *Müller*: Lyric Etude • *Ryba*: Little Invention • *Schytte*: Choral Etude; Springtime • *Türk*: I Feel So Sick and Faint, and more!
00119738 / $6.99

Second Grade

22 pieces: *Bartók*: The Dancing Pig Farmer • *Beethoven*: Ecossaise • *Bonis*: Madrigal • *Burgmüller*: Progress • *Gurlitt*: Etude in C • *Haydn*: Dance in G • *d'Indy*: Three-Finger Partita • *Kirnberger*: Lullaby in F • *Mozart*: Minuet in C • *Petzold*: Minuet in G • *Purcell*: Air in D Minor • *Rebikov*: Limping Witch Lurking • *Schumann*: Little Piece • *Schytte*: A Broken Heart, and more!
00119739 / $6.99

Third Grade

20 pieces: *CPE Bach*: Presto in C Minor • *Bach/Siloti*: Prelude in G • *Burgmüller*: Ballade • *Cécile Chaminade*: Pièce Romantique • *Dandrieu*: The Fifers • *Gurlitt*: Scherzo in D Minor • *Hook*: Rondo in F • *Krieger*: Fantasia in C • *Kullak*: Once Upon a Time • *MacDowell*: Alla Tarantella • *Mozart*: Rondino in D • *Rebikov*: Playing Soldiers • *Scarlatti*: Sonata in G • *Schubert*: Waltz in F Minor, and more!
00119740 / $7.99

Fourth Grade

18 pieces: *CPE Bach*: Scherzo in G • *Teresa Carreño*: Berceuse • *Chopin*: Prelude in E Minor • *Gade*: Little Girls' Dance • *Granados*: Valse Poetic No. 6 • *Grieg*: Arietta • *Handel*: Prelude in G • *Heller*: Sailor's Song • *Kuhlau*: Sonatina in C • *Kullak*: Ghost in the Fireplace • *Moszkowski*: Tarentelle • *Mozart*: Allegro in G Minor • *Rebikov*: Music Lesson • *Satie*: Gymnopedie No. 1 • *Scarlatti*: Sonata in G • *Telemann*: Fantasie in C, and more!
00119741 / $7.99

Fifth Grade

19 pieces: *Bach*: Prelude in C-sharp Major • *Beethoven:* Moonlight sonata • *Chopin*: Waltz in A-flat • *Cimarosa*: Sonata in E-flat • *Coleridge-Taylor*: They Will Not Lend Me a Child • *Debussy*: Doctor Gradus • *Grieg*: Troldtog • *Griffes*: Lake at Evening • *Lyadov*: Prelude in B Minor • *Mozart*: Fantasie in D Minor • *Rachmaninoff*: Prelude in C-sharp Minor • *Rameau*: Les niais de Sologne • *Schumann:* Farewell • *Scriabin*: Prelude in D, and more!
00119742 / $8.99

The brand-new *Classical Piano Solos* series offers carefully-leveled, original piano works from Baroque to the early 20th century, featuring the simplest classics in Grade 1 to concert-hall repertoire in Grade 5. The series aims to keep with the spirit of John Thompson's legendary *Modern Course* method by providing delightful lesson and recital material that will motivate and inspire. An assortment of pieces are featured, including familiar masterpieces by Bach, Beethoven, Mozart, Grieg, Schumann, and Bartók, as well as several lesser-known works by composers such as Melanie Bonis, Anatoly Lyadov, Enrique Granados, Vincent d'Indy, Theodor Kullak, and Samuel Coleridge-Taylor.

- The series was compiled to loosely correlate with the *Modern Course*, but can be used with any method or teaching situation.

- Grades 1-4 are presented in a logical and suggested order of study. Grade 5 is laid out chronologically.

- Features clean, easy-to-read engravings with clear but minimal editorial markings.

- View complete repertoire lists of each book along with sample music pages at **www.willispianomusic.com**.